First Selected Poems

First Selected
POEMS

LEO CONNELLAN

University of Pittsburgh Press

PS
3553
O5114
F5

9/1976
Am. Lit.

Library of Congress Cataloging in Publication Data

Connellan, Leo.
First selected poems.
(Pitt poetry series)
I. Title.
PS3553.05114F5   811'.5'4   75–29152
ISBN 0–8229–5268–8

Grateful acknowledgment is made to W. W. Davidson and Samuel J. Mandelbaum.

"Closed Wake" was first published in *Chelsea 24/25* (October 1968). "Dark Horses Rushing" first appeared in *The Georgia Review,* XXII, no. 1 (Spring 1968), © 1968 by the University of Georgia. "Lament for Federico Garcia Lorca," "The Moon Now Flushed," "Shadows," "Staten Island Ferry," "Helpless We Go Into This Ground, Helpless," and "Violent Dying" all appeared in *The New York Quarterly.* "Lobster Claw" and "Tell Her That I Fell" first appeared in *Steppenwolf.* "Watching Jim Shoulders" was first published in *The Nation.* "The Whole Thing About Jedge's House" was first published in *South and West.*

The publication of this book is supported

by a grant from the National Endowment for the Arts

in Washington, D.C., a Federal agency.

This book is for my wife, Nancy

CONTENTS

FROM Penobscot
Poems

LOBSTER CLAW

1

Morning and I
must kill.

Rise in one-bulb light, trying
to move quietly through
thin asbestos-braced house
shuddering at each of my steps,
the one-bulb light crashing
black dying night to
cowardly dawn, ashen at
our endeavor, so quiet
a twig snap jolts me,
as unwelcome suprise to all murderers.

Lobster, I will kill you now,
crouch in your rocks. Pull up
your bed covers of seaweed.
Ride the sea's bottom. Move
out deep in winter. Burrow
in mud. Hide under
kelp. I will bait you
to my family's survival
without conscience. My own
life is in the lines hauling you in.

The sea will rage to
upset my boat and have
you grabbing me in your
right crusher claw into
your efficient stomach
grinding up Mollusks, Algae,
and each other. But I
am a survived victim of
old storms. The ocean shrugs
at my approach.

I go, tired, braced
for you by determined
necessity, hope in me
that I can keep my
children from having to
laden their tables
by slaughter, fearing
I never can.

Lobster, let us
get this done. God
you must want me to
do this. Perhaps
the ocean with all its
bluff is not big enough
to keep all you lobster.

I will lay out a string of
redfish-baited traps you
cannot resist.

4

2

I am an old timer and
give my whole days.
Youngsters no longer
work the long hours, they
come in off the water early
and go to watch rooster-crowing
contests, fight and drink.

The sea is a womb, frothy
like blushing lovers are
shy, but within her,
after all, are the lives
of her many children
killing among themselves,
and she strikes down hard
those too naive to learn
that she is a sea not to be taken.

I am not easily caught,
but overwhelming fatigue
is my nemesis.

3

It is over, men like me
out in boats in the
great sea days. Airplanes
spot you now, lobster, scuba-divers
pluck you taking away your
choice to stay hidden
in ocean bosom, or
try to outwit the trap and
win the bait.

We were a breed of men
who could keep such
generated strength in our
sinews and wills as to
break the back of a bear
on a handful of food a
day and walk a hundred
miles, only our
open wilderness is the sea
with hoop net pots
made from iron tires
before Parlor traps, Double
Headers, long gaffing from
small boats on our
bleached-out green rock
coast, in blizzard winters,
endless fog summer days
dug into your bones and
never lets go a grip
that inner endurance must be
forged by us to survive,
until, as cow punchers
too long from women we
come in off our water
for fertility ritual and
blood.

4

Saturday night is
always our time. On the
sea we think of
our women, but mixed
in is the blood of good fights.

Nothing drives a man so
half out of his head as
work that never is enough
for his women and
children, never able
to give your woman
pretty things, your
youngsters something
better than lobstering,
our wind-burned lives
turned old, desperate.

Looking at our thin
frame houses, our pinched
women and our sons
will be out on the
boats with us soon, our
girls rushed to
the first men who
will support them,
whether there is love.

So, the boats in, tied
to their docks, an
edge of ice on the
evening wind, traps
piled to dry on
the wharves, we
walk by tourists come
to Clem's Pound,
picking their dinners
alive out of the day's
haul, frantic in
tanked salt water.

Home, our women
know there is no
stopping us, not
pouring all the liquor
their Baptist hearts
detest will mull
us from this
relished night.

5

There is a dance over to
South Thomaston, Postmaster's
son there from New York wearing
the city clothes of a
man who looks like
he never worked and
Woberton Edgecomb
walked over ready
to break his face
like hitting a glass
lampshade quick,
pulling your hand
back so fast you
don't skin a knuckle,
but the face
goes apart like
it never existed.

But they were talking
instead of going
at it, not
throwing a blow, him,
Postmaster's son
speaking soft, unriled
and damned if
he didn't reach out
and shake Woberton's
hand talking about
how they were through
high school together,
asking Woberton how
he'd been.

That was it! Out on
the sea, the ocean
sure don't ask you or
Clem paying us
grudgingly for our
lobster, but
Postmaster's son
was a Maine boy and
knew us, our
self-contained resentment.

But this here was
our Saturday
night to break heads,
ravish women for our
helplessness, our lives
always on the sea floating
and just then Elmer Tippett
come into South Thomaston
dance hall from Saint George,
the foreigner from
Houlton who'd married
his sister with him. None
of us liked the idea of
his having the little
Tippett girl. Houlton's
Potato country and we're
Lobstermen.

I know the pine trees shook
in their roots, when
Woberton Edgecomb turned
his punch meant for
Postmaster's son
and hit the Potato farmer
up off South Thomaston
dance floor like a
barn door struck by
a tractor.

But Potato fellas
can hit too, that's
the fun of it!

The getting the sea
and futility out
of you Saturday night
while your women wait
in thin frame houses
wondering how much
of you will have
to be put back together.

That Potato fella
was up at Woberton
and they were
spraying each other's
blood for their years.

11

I looked to take on
Postmaster's son
come visiting our hell,
then to go back
to his soft city life, the tourists
at Clem's Pound taking their
time selecting our
days' haul like cannibals
over their ruined prisoners,
turned me to murderous
hatred and right then
Postmaster's son would
have gone home in a
basket of my aggravation, even
if he did ask Woberton
how he was, but
Postmaster's son
was gone, using
the kind of brains
that escaped him from
the boats everyday life,
come home one time finally
busted apart, either
by a Saturday night
fight, Southern Comfort
full up back seat
auto fornication, or
the sea at last
too much to take on.

6

Lobster, colored
blue green, sky blue,
bright red, and even
albino, I'll find you.

I string my baited traps
each dawn and come after
them in the afternoon, and
the later I come back the
more of you lobster are
in them.

If you're "shorts," too small,
I throw you back, cursing
my waiting, my labor
for a lobster like you,
not big enough to bring
in and sell.

In the whole seas of
the world, Rockland, Maine,
is your home, lobster,
vulnerable shedding
your shell, helpless
as larvae floating
the ocean and later,
weak of your many
joints, claws, your
body easily snapped.

No one ever forgets the
sweet taste of lobster
claw meat driftwood
fire cooked beneath
steaming heaps of seaweed.

I must go out through
thick early morning
fog until sun burns
it off and I can
see. It is in this
darkness and then the
black of evening, when
I wearily ache, that I
could go wrong. So,
Morning I watch you,
and Evening, my eyes
are on you from noon.

Something I
did not consider, flame
near the boat's gas tank
could take me, and
it was the last thing
on my mind when
the blast threw me a
half mile all cut up
in pieces for you, lobster.

7

I'd rather finish
spitting at sea spray
that has slapped my
face fifty years,
than in some chair, but
my woman has spent
our lives waiting for
sundown when I
come into her arms.
Ocean, I owe her
some time and
Lobster you shall
not deny her.

No, Lobster, you shall
not have me. My
woman would like
to see once again
what I look like in
daylight for awhile
before we are no more
than the faces of clouds.

And all the heavy rain
down on lobstermen already
fighting the water that
is ocean, is our tears
weeping for knowledge
of him.

It is the sea mother
who whips him in a
wrath of wind like a
snarling cornered cat
while lobstermen
rip out her children.

So, to it then and
a day on the sea, fresh
wind and salt free
feeling. Tossing
the bowed trap, whichever
you think takes
strain best and I
take my chances on borers,
rather than risk
termite-treating
the traps and lose the
haul.

Morning again, and I must kill
to exist. Lobster,
scavenger crustacean,
why should I so mind
killing you!

TELL HER THAT I FELL

Woke me retching and alone.
Within doom booze
her arms around me again
in wished-for honeymoon time
that never happened.

Wait now to become ashes
and am so sorry.

Stagger now, shaking for what I'm running on.
But it takes a few to get started these days,
face gouged by razor unable fingers hold
and each step away from where a bar is near
makes me feel certain I'm going to drop dead.

Each morning now is terror.
The bathroom mirror reflects
earthworms have not a long wait
to pick me clean.
My toothpaste mouthwash
is a breakfast of liquor,
so is all day and every complete night.

Took her once in the snow
the seacoast near, vivid
like if bright red blood was blue.

Afterward when she stood up·
the bare spot we melted
was like two halves of a pear.

I know she is in a Fishing Village now
with many babies.
The boats go out each morning before sunup
breaks through salt fog and come in long after dark,
just to make ends meet.

Maybe he is good to her
in his clumsy understanding
I hope so, but never sure in his mind.
Furiously suspicious at any man's glance at her,
eternally looking for whoever I am
directly into the face of each tourist who comes
into town.

How it frustrates him, unable
to find and strangle me
who is always the wedge between his best effort,
and he is so strong, sea life hardened.

Wake me these days retching then, all right
just tell her that I fell.
My happiness time was with her,
been any kind of a man
I would have carried her like
a knapsack away and felt
her feet slapping my thighs.

Come on, death, I fear
to wobble the few steps to you.

DARK HORSES RUSHING

Mathew Brady
        there's an old shack now
                by the stones
with auto tires hung on nails
        below 7-UP signs and from inside
the nasal adenoid indigestion-giving
              holla of Bob Dylan.

But I swear, Mat, just as I pulled
        into the Filling Station,
              Dylan shut off a minute,
and I could hear horses riding hard
        like death in pursuit of itself.

Ages now, Mathew Brady,
        have accomplished Infrared camera
we can point at a group of rocks
        insignificant now alongside
super eight-lane highway
        driving up through the breasts
of Georgia to the moon in her crown.

Near Infrared, closer catching image
            left by body's heat
will show up a ghost to my great-granddaughter
            where a corn-haired Confed boy sat
on those stones asleep in the dream of his lady
            and the blue-coat boy shot him dead
standing up like a despicable Fox hunter
kicked out of the lair for a week
            in birth of baby fox time,
big wide grin on his face wiped out
            by a good three-hundred-yard shot
that took measuring the wind by the eye
            of Confed buddy over yonder
and gunsmoke choked the tears out of leaves.

Then dark horses rushing
            inside thunder
as both sides scattered
            for the life God gives us once.

WATCHING JIM SHOULDERS

When did my manhood wake to its dying!
Never in New England or in Elko, Nevada, inside
screen doors with legal girls, dulled by fifty-cent splits.
But in Colorado's air and snow like first communion lace on
blunt mountains. He was Mantle on horseback, the
same class, and as injured, out of that remote private
America of ranges, ranches, vast wide-open space where
sophistication is silence. Truth is your action shot
from corrals, lasso wrist flicked instantly with
eight seconds to rope and tie or lose. Shoulders,
scraping the cheeks of steers along earth cut by
grooves of his boot heels, while those horns that could
cave in ribs, turned until the folds in the animal's
neck looked like its spine would split through skin,
yet didn't in this master's hands.

SHADOWS

I cannot look at birds or hear
them singing. We failed
to be men in the flood of our youth,
how can we ever be old men!
We will be shadows, shells
of carcasses rocking on porches
until the wind explodes us
and we are the foul smell
in the air turning the noses
of lovers and children, in
some vague future peace time.
I have nodded to God and
He looked right through me.

CLOSED WAKE

Silence, I am seeking quiet.
My insides no longer burst to flowers
or hay like the smell of sun
on the back of your hand.

My foot smacked rivers,
and I paddled canoes on pure water,
before defecating boats, until
animals would not come to drink.

We packed our bags for a planet,
leaving only tombstones.

After exhausting calcareous tissue
of all the slaughter, we dug Indians up,
shipping their bones to make buttons.
Now computers stalk us.

I love the woods. All the
wilderness is come down.
We are in cages of mortar.
Our open plains become skid rows
of the flood tide of penises
until cactus needles wilt.
If we had only used our brains instead.

A HEN CROSSING A ROAD

Frenzied Sunday dinner
sensing the way we size her up
with the sensuous look of anticipating pigs
waiting to wallow our faces in her flesh.
Bobs, weaves, back and forth
from the yard gravel too near the chopping block;
darts no straight path across
the old dusty dirt pebbled road and comes back
noncommittal, flapping courageous wings.
When the Ax falls
refuses to be dead until she has run her blood out.

OLD GRAVESTONES

See them in morning mist like fingernails of
some gigantic hand ripped up
through the hard ground trying with some unseen
massive shoulder ripple thrown through dirt to
get them all back on earth to live. Death was so
quick. In the old cemetery chipped slate bent like
loose teeth in this head of earth. The short years
on the stones. Infants hardly out of the womb, dead.
Now the world moves too fast. Man is down to his
last breath and his youngsters, with graveyards
staring at them, stalk tombstones, enraged,
wandering in among our sanctified history that we
treasure in our fear of oblivion. Carved angels
with halos and wings, legends chiseled into stone
that prove we are immortal here on earth forever, but
in rage, in raging anger our young kick them down,
descecrate, destroy the preserved memory of vanished
men, in rage against quick dismissal by us into
earth forever with an old gravestone all that's
left of them.

OLD ORCHARD BEACH MAINE
BURNED DOWN

Fire has leveled my baby's toyland.
We are father and child in the same place.
It was my playpen too, Sea Weed beach
and the sense of salt and sand on
you and sunburn.

Town of Merry-Go-Round and Donkey cart
rides in dark underground tunnels through
the wonders of horror, down a simulated
mine shaft full of ogres that leaped out
at you. Ferris Wheels town of fun. Children
town burned down. Town of glee-filled laughing
youngsters and hideout motels for lovers right
over the beach. Town of people growing old
on their last time around.

Town for me once when I was young, and
I yearn to go back there now. Town a hurricane
ripped apart in my youth, throwing the Merry-Go-
Round I knew in my boyhood like a scaled saucer,
gone, as we took our only child back where I was
once happy, to a Merry-Go-Round in flames when
Old Orchard Beach Maine burned down, from a
heater too near dry wood and the wind was right.
Again all gone but the scent of fresh pine on
the sea's wind.

                                       turned back pages in an ancient
black and molded photo album, yellowing snapshots of
a chubby dark-curled boy and an equally chubby
light-curled boy in what were pinafore suits seated
on the sunny sand beside two huge-hatted choker-
dressed women . . . Aunt Annie and Mamma with the
spindly O O Pier poles and Casino in back, around 1916,
Jim Moore of Glen Cove, Maine, remembers and writes this poet,
. . . in another photo, dad, shirt sleeves rolled up onto
elastics and pant legs rolled to the knees, barefooted with

us boys . . and in a brown-covered, less molded book, some
earlier Jim Moore girl friends who got waitress and
Chamber jobs at some of the inns, with the same pier in back,
while still later, yes, a couple more blondy beaned boys looking
at the wonders of the old steam peanut machine engine and
cart at the inboard end of the Pier . . . Moore's own kids . . .

What child imagines his own child!
I remember walking these streets, a
boy with no idea that flesh I helped make
would one day love this place too and
be visible in front of my eyes on my memory
back when once I ran ragged swam this sea by
Googins rocks until bleary-eyed exhausted in
happiness, I could no more, but only sleep.

                                        dancing out on the pier that fell down.
the old pier with its underpinnings
crammed into sand for fifty years
holding up the ballroom where the
big bands played out over the ocean.

                    There was a luncheonette on the
                    corner of East Grand Avenue that
                    served big thick mayonnaise pickle
                    crab-meat sandwiches squirting out
                    the side of the bread.

                    And perfect rainy movie days,
                    a swim in the warm sea with rain
                    falling on you and dry feeling smooth
                    as a pearl from the ocean swim, into
                    see Brian Donlevy playing "Heliotrope Harry."

Gone, its all gone, the town's still there, there
is a beach and ocean still, but it belongs to someone
else, the French Canadians, starving for a sea,
Old Orchard Beach Maine is gone for my

daughter too, at six she looked at me, at
only six and said out of her mouth
—"It will never be the same," yes, a six-
year-old said that, she meant they rebuilt
but not the fun games she loved, and she
knew it at only age six, they're gone, all
but the ocean, its all changed but the
never-ending sea-pounding ocean in Old
Orchard Beach Maine, like a woman you loved
once and can't give up because she's old
and ruined, run down and lived in, but
it will never be the same with her any more,
however you look at her and love comes
back to you . . . love for her, you loved
her once, you couldn't catch your breath for her.

OUT JIM MOORE'S WINDOW

Out Jim Moore's window,
in the living room of his house in Glen Cove, Maine,
stealing this visit like a dart on a boomerang,
my blue Atlantic boyhood scrutinizes me off
the slip borders of the Penobscot across Strawberry Hill.

See through glass, over Jim's Patio back lawn,
tough fading green that light went out of from salt,
the beautiful water of the cove unchanged.

I remember the boy who looked out on that Sea water
knowing it would take him to the world,
to blind all this in his accomplishment.

All come back to me here
in the silence of maturity's afternoon.
Things go wrong. We fail.

I am no longer bursting juice skinny youth,
but a man staggered by risks. Yet back across Kittery bridge,
things to do still must be
and I can't come home until they're done.

FROM The Gunman
and Other Poems

THIS IS A STICK-UP

El Welfare Chevito slunk out of his urine stench Casa
to feed a needle to the fella sitting down on the nerve ends of his
    bowels
like some impaled Prime Minister slipping his feet on a greasy pole
where he can get up off and can't.

Evening just turned dark touched lovely people like you and me
with soft caressing breezes, but El Welfare Chevito like a victim of
    croton oil.
Crave jabbed murder onto his relief-screeching brain. Pastrami-gorged
    police
sitting on the wide buttocks of no exercise, waited to get their sex with
    six guns.

And up the avenue innocent victim in the white apron of piety
that concealed the one-eighth worth of Virginia ham he gave you after
you paid him for half a pound, made the slot man at the Daily Spread
    Eagle
his morning headlines for the big shots laying cents down for a copy
like it was nothing.

It was over in a minute, light flashed on light
throwing the good guy's glasses off his sneak thief's suprised eyes
stamped with a gasp muffled by his shoulders hitting groceries
falling all over him like stir crazy cons leaping hopelessly nowhere.

But outside, slinking up with their winking whore's light
to kill forever the seed of a life, the wide blue bottoms
had El Welfare Chevito blasted into street with so many holes in him
it was hard to get in a last dream of faraway Puerto Rico.

ON THE EVE OF MY BECOMING A FATHER

I have turned now in the night and
all my blown-away kisses of our familiar love
with the words and sillinesses
always thrust by nature's drive,
lost in the loneliness of our sighs
in the dark, in darkness even with
blazing lights on and booze
to slobber down our failure
so we could turn on our pillows
as if we did not know each other.
We had been every place but this
and our travel folders were worn out.
I had been about to hang up my gun
but the hammer shot one spark into the moon,
so magnificent, it is beyond me.

AS AN APPLE HAS IRON

Astronauts, jumping stars like stream pebbles
into the sun's blood yoke, we are all travelers
if risk is proven removed, but now you cannot
open your enclosed faces on, say, Venus of sweet
confidence, "the beautiful white one," "the
mistress of the heavens." I had hoped as Galileo,
that beneath Venus bed covers of clouds lay a virgin
Brazil, a new place to begin fresh like Australia
once, America, for the world grows weary, but all
oxygen of Venusian oceans lies locked in rusty
planet surface, the air we need to live immediately
taken by the iron to become rust as here on earth
an apple has iron and bitten into, exposed by our
teeth, opened to oxygen becomes rusty brown and dies.

What will we find of the Moon or Mars and the others,
Astronauts who cannot step out of their get-ups to find
it anything smells like rich green new grass of an
earth spring rain. You are curiosities pitted
against the impossible.

MUNDELEIN ON THE MICHIGAN

Great blue and lake birds
skimming night off dawn
with the fingernail of a quarter moon,
when I am alone with early morning
as it slips off its black gown.

Out of bed with the morning awake,
it is in this new hour of days
that I am my best and there is
Lake Michigan like a trapped big tear.

I came in on a plane fresh
from shadows and angles
where my moves are to survive, screaming the
condition of a bumblebee down an air shaft.

And my heart knows the anguish we must control.
I will go and be gone and your fresh beauty will be
for others, damned as I am to
cry for the wounds that break us.

Bird squadrons low over the water
yellow, gray, white, blue, according
to sun shades and wind spray, but
it is not my life, I am the
wolf with a lamb in his teeth,
why did God turn me around!

OF THE BETRAYED

I give you ashes.
No one can find
which dust is your son.

No young girl will ever lift
the blankets of darkness delighted
at his sword in her.

No young child will ever
pinch a nipple of his breasts.

No young girl will ever cry
he left her.

No young child will finally
stammer the word father
to his proud hearing.

No, we will not have these things
to concern ourselves of him
and I will never have him either
nor you, nor anyone. He
is the fertilizer of grass.

Yes, I remember him,
he came in with sideburns
to his jawbones. First
we took his wavy hair, then
innocence out of his eyes
and stamped death into the pupils.

We robbed him of his chance on
the earth, turned him on his
fellow man, so that he undoubtedly
felt he had the explosion coming
that stained his knees with his life.

He hated us in heartbroken weeping,
not knowing any more than you do
where he was going when
he closed his eyes and could not open them.

I give you his ashes
mingled with others.
See them, can't you see them!

FROM *Another Poet in New York*

LAMENT FOR FEDERICO GARCIA LORCA

In the early dawn bleak cold
without sunlight,
They smashed the Butterfly
against a wall.

Yes, I know we are only children,
children picking up the smatterings
of what we can.

That brutal morning
the capes of Spain
folded themselves in shame.

We are children
who were not there,
know nothing of it.

But there are those among us
who even while we are children
put the eyes out of kittens,
tie Cats' tails together and
toss them over a clothesline
feeling warm pleasure
witnessing their frantic clawing
each other to death.

We will be the ones
who will do it again.

In all likelihood
the boys among us
will grow up and marry the girls
trying endlessly to prove our manhood.

Some of us never can.
We will always think it is in question,
that all eyes focus on us as un-men.

We will murder anyone
who does not feel a need to prove it,
is such a voice that birds
stop in flight in air to listen.

He is the veins
in which Spain's Conquistadores' blood
reached its bouquet.

His precious singing words
of such magnitude
they clutch our breath.

Yes, I know we are only children,
children picking up the smatterings
of what we can.

He was whisked out of his house
as dawn was breaking,
his eyes deprived of one more sun
before forever dark.

Killed because he
wore skirts in the heart of his trousers.

We will let it happen again,
when the time comes
some of us will do it.

We are children
who could see to it, it did not
but we will not.

Would not want to be of them
who smashed the Butterfly against a wall
and the Courvoisier of his mind
wasted forever at only age thirty-six.

Whatever is the good to talk to children
who will do it again.

Federico, Garcia, Lorca . . . some of us
some of us are heartbroken. . . .
They do not make enough candles
in all the world's churches
to burn for you.

Not enough Rosaries can be said
or Acts of Contrition.

Because I know
it will happen again.

CONSCIOUS

Amphisbaena, go me East
and slip among the unconcern.
There, and come back here win,
because I know how to kill.
And yet melt excited upon even
just seeing Margot Fonteyn
or a Dandelion for that matter,
white puffed coming apart in the
brutal air.

MOMMY'S HUBBY

We were drinking buddies in high old time town
womb warm with Billie songs and Bird jazz,
so I put you up when you asked me now, but
you blew it when I filled the refer Ale full against my wife's frown.

　　　　She has seen me like we were
　　　　and my marriage cartwheeled for a minute.

　　　　　　Hey, buddy, the wind avoids
　　　　　　flashing his cape of zest at me.

How come you think the chicks still die downstairs for Jackie Levine!?
Jackie Levine has shot his last load in a young head.

　　　　　　Jackie, Jackie Levine, Captain U.S. Cavalry
　　　　　　Falling all over the Pacific, leaving his wife
　　　　　　to finger herself, with a glue hairdo
　　　　　　up in perpetual pin curlers,
　　　　　　America's love-starved sweetheart dried up like a prune
　　　　　　being true to Jackie Levine, dashing warrior.

And the mandolins were playing for hard-nose Fisk.
his red nose shines a medal from all the whiskey companies,
but the bottles are all broken in city dumps
full of Seagulls and stink.

　　　　　　Our youth went out in tapped beer-keg blasts,
　　　　　　spread-legged chicks where are you, wives of
　　　　　　upstate doctors taking it on your sun decks
　　　　　　behind shrubbery concealing freeways?

　　　　　　You liked it in an East Side dump
　　　　　　giving your cries to old men
　　　　　　through cockroach paper-thin walls.

And I am Willis Fisk again
creeping streets to my job and crawling home.

It gets over sometime, when?
why do we wait!

We wait waiting to find out what we waited for,
then we're quite willing to leave.

Hey, buddy, you remember that sweet young thing
come into Johnny Romero's on Minetta with oranges for a nice
tight little ass so pot high she didn't know who you was next
morning after we both banged her so drunk we never knew if
we got off or not and she looked at us through her shades
like we were creeps.

Hey, buddy, remember Jerry's on the Bowery
where I'd get a three-day kick washin' dishes and after
fly for Thunderbird and Fanny'd come by with a bottle of
green gin and maybe money to blot out horrible Sunday and
you'd turn on your charm talkin' until finally dawn . . .

I remember, sure I do.
I lie awake seeing it
in the snore dark of marriage.

Now, you come to my house as though Billie was still singin' "Easy Living,"
The Bird still blowin' in high old time town.

In the face of my old lady who saw me through
all the galloping hee-hee's,
well, Jackie Levine, I have to say so long.

Yes, it's Fisk tellin' you split.
Imagine it, Fisk tellin' you leave!
Because now I'm Mommy's Hubby and we've got our coffins picked out
plots and perpetual flowers.

THE MOON NOW FLUSHED

Across America the
young men were
throwing their
serial numbers away,
and some were sticking
their thumbs out along
the highways hitting
the cities broke.

And always Fry Cook
and Counterman jobs in
the cafeteria chains or
loading freight cars
with empty beer cans at
the American Can company.

You learned to buy and
carry with you your own
skillet that scrambled eggs
would never stick in, which
could put you out of work,
and a small pot for poached
eggs, your own equipment,
black tie and cummerbund so
you could get into a town
like Seattle with your girl
with you, put her some place,
in just a room to start, walk
into a spoon and go right to
work if there was any
job as a waiter,
dishwasher, counterman,
fry cook. Meant an
immediate meal for you,
meant money now.

The whole world hadn't
exploded. Boiling, but
the roads were still open
and the young girls
like the exciting kernels
of corn to strip their
green stalks down.

Blood of my dreams, I just
thought I saw you again when
the moon now flushed
across the pane of my window glass.

Now the daffodils were pushing
their daisies. It was the
last hour that blacks cringed.
My boyhood went when you did.

The last time blacks shook, yes,
before, I'm hip, they got wise
to why the old revolutionaries
tagged themselves Yankee,
Yankee Doodle and the sharpest
blacks realized all at once,
like all sudden realization,
that their pride lies in Nigger,
the tag to shout, to give themselves
back, Nigger like Yankee Doodle went
to town and Nigger he went too,
is going to town.

The cities were not yet exploding
in violence. Young men seeking
their women, blood of my life.
The grief of thinking of you now
almost shuts off my breath.

Going through girls to
find you. Neither of us knew
that love is taking punishment
while giving the other hell.

Young good-looking black men with
megaphone voices drank themselves
to death because no black could get
any part in our freckle-faced
strawberry blond cinema.

Young men looking to
find themselves and blood,
blood of my blood, young women
looking to be found. Where
was I for you.

Destroyed before we met.
You could not know that.
Why were you on the road too,
available. Road people are
usually losers or have dreams
and are trying to get away
from the death of staying home.
Your own mother and father destroy
you, no enemy, no stranger,
but the flesh that put you on earth.

I was violated in my boyhood
by the tip your forelock terror,
fear, my parents' fear of their jobs,
place in the community if any
child of theirs tried to become
a Poet or Ballerina or Actress.

Who did you think you were!
You ought to beg for a
file-clerk job in
the telephone company.

Screamed into you and
broke you, broke your heart
broke your ambitions, your
initiative and made you
overweight or in a hospital
or in drink.

The dead cannot regret
and a man like me
cannot either.

I was no one to go with
in the first place. But
once you came with me I
was no one to leave.

Freeloader of the sit-down girls who
do nothing. Who put out and go, flit
back and forth, never stay anywhere,
anybody's make. Lesbian meat too.
Before you are through you will be kept
by women once all the men are
wise to you and the hills of that
fantastic backside are starting to cave in.

Then a woman in bed on you or
you in bed on a woman will be better
than in darkness alone. You will
think of me then. You will often
think of me. I often thought of
you in cheap rooms when I had
no money and no woman.

I confess, I do not comprehend women.
They cling. All most men want is to
bust, feel good and be free. Women
know this, know they would be thrown out
until it was time to play with the
erector set again. The nest
builder has to capture a provider
or he'll seed her and be gone. I
have made few women happy long.
I make love to them and lose them.

The women who have known me, felt
the strong massage of my gripping
fingers manipulating their pimple-
speckled turkey carcasses best, can
say if I am more at home with men. You
will find me in a woman every time
you discover me in pitch dark, a
woman will be in my arms.

But do I ever really
remember the woman
for who she is or
only how I used her.

You fall in love with a good blow job.
The face of the lips gets to you. The
eyes looking up at you need to be told
you love them, and she does it so good she
wins your heart. Suddenly you want
all of her. You feel
you are going crazy.
It was so uncomplicated.
Now, where would you ever
find another woman who
would let you kill her

every day. You come to
think that she likes it.
Only it's crazy, she
leaves you.

She liked it. Nothing on
earth keeps doing what it
detests and she went down
right to it. She liked it,
or the only way to do what
you can't stand is to plunge
and get to it. Then, she
did it for fear of losing me
if she didn't. Imagine my
losing her.

Imagine! You left me in front
of the old Cafe Riviera, the
one Andy and Al ran in
New York City. You left me
drunk on the sidewalk. A man
you had held in your arms. You
left me drunk and mumbling,
realizing you were going. You
would not hear me beg you
not to leave me. You even
dressed up to say good-bye to me,
I remember how we were, how
poor we were, yet you managed
a cheap dress and high heels to say
good-bye to me. I had it coming.
But I wanted you. You were some
beautiful girl. You are as lost
as I am and you did the best
you could. You were willing
to do anything with me to try
to find happiness yourself.

What can I say, I can't say
your name any more. I know
I had something when I was
with you.

I couldn't stop you from going.
I know the slobbering was an
act in my hooked cowardice of
how I expected I should look
like I was feeling about
your leaving me there on
the sidewalk in front of
everybody, when I was a
drunk gratefully relieved
of not having to cope with
you, the keeping of you
any more . . . wouldn't it be
nice to be able to rave
betrayed, betrayal from you.
You were untrustworthy.
No one knew where you were
liable to be or do, but
you betrayed no one. I
betrayed you. You stood me
past the limit of your
limited abilities.
You were yourself.

Blood of my heart, often I
will wake suddenly in the
night and see you coming to me.

Now here fitted together
the green window shade of our youth
is pulled down.

Water is falling on your gasp
off my brow.

But you will leave me and
years come I cannot forget you.

Love, my lover, why did you go,
why did you leave me so alone.
We were a pair.

Where will you be and will you
suddenly start, as a shadow in
the fallen evening hits your mirror,
makes your face drain ashen at that
moment realizing it took two people to part.

Across America the young boys
were let loose, when the niggers
stagnated in their juice for the
last time and the young yellows
poised to erupt on San Francisco
in the waning patience of the
young reds. Now the girls are
all emancipated. I wonder if they
will be any better to males, than
men have ever been to women.

THE WHOLE THING ABOUT JEDGE'S HOUSE

Across from the stadium in Jerome's cafeteria
we have just come from defacing monuments;
slurp our coffee feeling nervous
before taking the downtown train
to being nobody.

After the ball game, we walked jammed ramps
past bronze plaques to Gehrig,
Huggins and Jedge.
Some of us marked up their faces
in vicious compulsion
to cut down our betters,
our shoes covered
with the light orange cinders they walked in.

We said we loved them.
They look at us now scratched,
in the rain, in the sunlight.
Permanently mutilated
is our love for them.

We are the pot-bellied chuck-a-beers,
peanuts out of the shell in our rotten teeth,
with the foul stench
of gulped Hot Dogs on our breath.
Wounded animal whine from inside us rises
into shrieks over replanted
Kentucky bluegrass
like a huge card table with midgets.

Pitcher dealing from a huge
cut out of the green
to Catcher set for any action
like a Gunslinger.

In close Bagmen with a Shortstop to
pop the balloon of a hit.

Player comes to bat and as Pitcher moves,
mannequin triangle fielders fold
jackknife blades ready from a slingshot
to get that ball.

A Mantle is many things, a
Mantle is a cloak.
We can look at our sons remarking,
see, the old man
might have something left in him yet.

When Mickey hit he clobbered death.
Missing, his hand formed
as a Swan on a fishhook pulling greatness
vanished into the dugout again
in Jedge's house.

STATEN ISLAND FERRY

For a nickel the man
from the lower East Side
can ride the ocean.

Away from the skyline's
exhausted face, chiseled into
and blown apart for new
cheekbone features of glass buildings
rising above cold steel where
killers of people sprung from
the jobless traps, struggling
to take and rotting for it
in Attica.

The ocean-going liner
of people who have nothing.
Below decks on the long
rows of endless rigid
wood bench seats, poor
kids hug and tongue-kiss,
imagine! The only place
you have to try to make
love, a foul-smelling, dead-
cigar-stinking cold
Ferry boat.

The boy kid looks
like he's nothing
getting something.

As you walk by
the girl's big eyes
look apprehensive, but
her mouth is still on
his mouth, and he's
sprawled back with
his shirt loose out of
his trousers showing his
lean naked hard-muscled
wiry body, and he is
stiff down his left pant
leg, letting her work
herself up, like he's
out on his own private boat.

She makes you sense
that he's all she's got
and she's beside herself
trying to keep him,
even to letting the
public watch.

Filthy old sweaty boat,
sweat-encaked and hungry
Sea Gulls drilling the
Hudson of its refuse.

For a nickel you walk a deck
as though you can dream
you aren't a messenger and
don't pull a hand truck through thieves
grabbing a box out of your
too loosely tied hand truck load,
timed just as a bus stops and
the robber gets on and is
gone fast to his fence.

While you're trembling in gratitude
that he didn't knife or shoot you,
you're going to get home another
time tonight! . . . For a nickel out
on the Staten Island Ferry
you are rich, privileged to
go and come on the sea. Once
I knew a girl, beautiful like
a tulip, who climbed up in the cab
with the horny driver
and pulled his cord for him
that blew the whistle on them.

We had all been looking over
at Elizabeth, New Jersey,
when she honked our eyes
up to her wriggling around on his knees.

On our way to Staten Island, going
past the Lady from France, what
a dream! How easily man
forgets what he has
fought for and won, but
worse, his children,
not knowing what we went through,
give away the free breath we
got them with our lives. I love
you, lady with the torch and
all the corn that I believe in
because I like to go and come
as I please, unregimented and
without fear . . . like on the
Staten Island Ferry and off it
at my whim.

Staten Island, old graveyards,
back country roads so near the city,
and on the Staten Island Ferry a
feeling of reeling power that
a city should have such a
Ferry boat of Ellis Island dreams
after the big bridges, spanning
boroughs like a hand with
spread fingers on its wealth.

Yes, for a nickel anyone can feel
he has something that is his, alone.
For five cents you go on this boat out
across the harbor where
New York City stands at attention for you.

HELPLESS, WE GO INTO THIS
GROUND, HELPLESS

> Across the bridges and under the earth,
> subway trains lumber and clank.

Helpless, we go into this ground, helpless
each day packed against each other so that
we always start off irritable
at being tossed about thrown against strangers.

People who never get to know each other
but ride the train every day
without ever exchanging dreams.

> The subway screeches
> ear piercingly through tunnels
> and rattles into the station
> like an undone Accordion.

The whole subway train shudders
as it stops. The train doors
open like gasping mouths.

> And we get on staggering
> shadows of giants, forced
> to become Subway Passengers,
> pushing, shoving, we are made
> into something else than human
> in this insult, cramming against each
> other in our own foul exhale.

> In the subway water
> always falling off
> station walls as though
> the held-back rivers
> will break through over us.

Here we are flushed out
of our anonymity.

> To whom do we look good?
> Villon, did you do that!

61

We get on the same train
every morning for years
and usually the same car.

                    Through the earth and on the bridges
                    subway trains groan. . . .

We get off the train
and go a hundred
different directions
to our daily fates.

We get on the same train
every morning, surviving
the subway each day as
prisoners do, disassociating
from what was . . . and is . . .
and will be . . .

                But, Subways I
                defeated you.

               Overwhelming Subways I
               hung on.

I climbed, climbed, climbed
your endless straight-up
stairs back out to sunshine.

Helpless, we go into this ground, helpless
onto dank, dark, brutally cold
impartial platform to wait
for trains that throw our insides around
until panic seizes and you gasp
in terror that you might suffocate,
with the scribblings of restrained
psychotics on everything, the walls, posts,
train windows, all over the trains in
insulting thumb noses at us vulgar orange, purple

which the rest of unstable us who somehow
cope must add to what we endure. We
let them draw on us, rather than slaughter us.

But there is no such help for us,
if we suddenly blow it's Bellevue
or one of those unfortunate assassinations
by the good-guy off-duty cop who just happened
to be on his way home with a well-loaded gun ready
for us, because we aren't ghetto kids
in the amnesty of invisible veiled threat to
go wild in our condition.

We go helpless down into this ground, helpless,
can you imagine getting stalled underground,
the subway train coming to a full stop down
deep in the earth in ninety-nine-degree heat,
the train stops and the sickening
scent of burning wood . . .

                    Off the bridges and into the earth
                    gouged out for it the subway train stalls.

Helpless, down in the ground, we are under
the earth now in company of people we don't
know . . . helpless into this ground, helpless.

We have resigned ourselves wrecks to them,
these shattering, jarring subway trains that
we must take or not go anywhere.

VIOLENT DYING

In Thanksgiving week of a cold poverty year
two men came in to rob a bar and
the gunman shot everybody.

New York, for you to let death loose
like this! New York what have you become
that you have a sewer smell of death.

New York, green in its dirt.
East River already floating dead to the sea.
And the Hudson dying of garbage
at our lady in the harbor's feet.

You are a thousand simultaneous actions,
in my system unlike the frighteningly
ordered cities, like a charwoman's best effort.

Humanity rushing up the underlining
of your belly to be spit out at their doors.

Starving men look bewildered
at High Rises across from their hunger.

A doormat is liable to be a human being
down at the bottom of the doorsteps of dying
in Manhattan, in New York.

You are a city where
a man could kill himself and lie dead
until he exploded through his orifices
and his blood fall down on his neighbors,
not knowing what agency to call.

New York, weren't you my lover, New York?
Weren't you!? Didn't you take me into
your arms? Weren't we hungry together.

Do you kill your lover grown old,
a little gray and fat, but look in my eyes.
They are the cold steel of two bulls
that have put horns in all the matadors.

And I made you scream once and then die.
When you woke up I was gone. Now I will
not come to you again, because if I do
you will kill me.

Death in your doorways, death
across the street exploding and blowing
heads off, death a little tiny blade
slipping into ribs, death
with the sour smell of burnt powder.

We are helpless in blinding sunlight
now in you, New York.

Your shadows are full
of merciless slaughter.

Who stops plunging the blade to
ask if you are Einstein! Who stops
if you are, who stops simply because
you are another human being who
does not wish to be struck down.

Death did not always seem to hover
on us. There were years some vague
world war one veteran uncle, your
mother's brother, stuck away in a
perpetual bathrobe always over his
beer and cribbage, that the family
whispered was mustard gassed, who
always looked at you through the
thick bifocals of his great injury,
was the only thing about death
you knew; your skin crawled around
him who had left his Altar Boy blessing
himself at all the Thou Shall Not Kill
masses, to kneel and receive communion
on his tongue before Infantry charges,
it seemed with God's blessing, while

he shoved his bayonet into man stomachs
and sudden frightened surprise blew
life out of those eyes as he followed
each bayonet plunge by pulling the
trigger and then forward and forward and
Oh My God I Am Heartily Sorry For Having
Offended Thee and then all the
world in his own ears.

How do you tell a lovely girl you
want to marry you that you kill
easily crossing yourself, blessing
it away, running with a herd of killers
with the wafer of God still dissolving.

New York death is
all over you.

Death is on your tall buildings
and death is in the streets.

The air we breathe
death.

Death now not death that
kills children who run in front of cars.

Death, murder, New York and I cannot
come in to you to be killed.

The Red Knight could go to him
jaunty with a flair and scarf
aimlessly in flames, but death
should not be for people come
into a bar to have drinks and birthday cake.

A girl turning thirty-nine reluctantly, bought
birthday cake to bring in to shake
routines, not to die.

Common, bars crowded with desperate
victims of the Manhattan trap, cold,
roach-filled apartment off hallways stenched
with the urine of a hundred years.

Despair drives the young who do not
grasp full meanings and penalties to
use up their own lives.

Because when you walk in and shoot everybody
you're going away forever.

Two men come in to rob and the
gunman shot everybody.

His companion begged him not to but
death had climbed into his skin, who
was no longer the old death of chivalry
you had to go find, but a
life seeker and a life taker.

The other man covering all of them in the bar;
How terror clutched them as they
dreaded, hoped and dared not move.

I know that professional killers can't
fleece you if you're dead, but only pick
your cold pockets, I know their butchers
get obliterated, Joe Jelly, who would corner
you and enjoy your helpless wriggling to live
as he put on white dress gloves and told you
that if you were nice and didn't resist he'd
put a quick one in your heart, but if you
gave him trouble he'd kill you slow,
so you'd roll around and think about it.

This gunman's companion begged him not to flash
death around like that, but he did not
shoot him to stop him, although murderer either way.

He didn't point his weapon at him and command
that they call the whole thing off or take the
money but call off death. No, he stood there begging
his companion not to do it but let him do it.

And murder was inside
the gunman's trigger finger.

He could be any of our sons, there are no
heroes home from wars these days.

What death can do to a man
to make him a killer of life
that never did a thing to him.

Killer, did you go over to war decent, but
they cut off ears in front of your eyes, they
wanted your insides cold to screams. They
brought out a beautiful young girl, tied her
between poles and made you watch them
pour gas on her and light it.

How could you come home and tell us that
we had violated you, taken away joy
from you forever.

How could you ever again be with a woman
without seeing her ablaze, your
children without ears.

So, you just walked into a bar
and the hunting license
is out on us all now.

I can no longer come into New York
out of my Connecticut cocoon.

If I sneeze and quickly reach
into my trenchcoat for kleenex
a thousand police guns will kill me.
They will have heard the bark of my nose
and my dying ears will hear their guns explode.

Good-bye, New York, New York of Hart Crane and
William Packard, New York of Garcia Lorca, New
York of Allen Planz. New York of my young manhood
held in your hand and blown over your harbors of
polluted death, good-bye greatest of the world's
cities, good-bye, I love you but good-bye.

AUTUMN

Brown, brown leaves,
brown strangled orange.
Brown orange stiff turned in cold air
to crumble and disappear.
Cider scent on the wind
blowing its breath on mud ruts
into congealed reflections
holding summer for a look.

First Selected Poems

Leo Connellan

Leo Connellan, out of a vigorous and, at times, difficult life, has been making powerful poems for twenty-five years. This is the first selection from all of his work to be published — a significant event in American poetry.

His work has been praised by other veteran poets:

"I do like this book — and how much more poetry here than in most of the books I have read for a year ... for one thing, the emotional 'build,' control, and the rhythmical effects in 'Out Jim Moore's Window' and what a marvelous end for a poem in the last two lines of 'Shadows.'" — Robert Penn Warren

"'Lobster Claw' is probably my favorite of all the poems ... and the Lorca is just as good. 'Violent Dying' is powerful. [Connellan is] one of the few people who can hold up a long poem." — Karl Shapiro

"Everybody interested in modern poetry should read the passionate work of Leo Connellan. He speaks with the authority of experience, profound knowledge of the heart, and a deep realization of man's predicament. His poetry is vital and strong." — Richard Eberhart

"There is a wiriness in the movement of these poems that I like. There are many powerful pieces." — Richard Wilbur

Leo Connellan lives with his wife and daughter in Clinton, Connecticut, where he is a sales representative for a stationery firm. He has received grants for his writing from the National Endowment for the Arts and the State of Connecticut Commission on the Arts and has recorded his poetry for the Library of Congress.

University of Pittsburgh Press